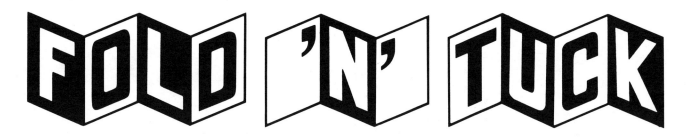

FOLD 'N' TUCK

STEVE BRODNER

A DOLPHIN BOOK

DOUBLEDAY

NEW YORK LONDON TORONTO SYDNEY AUCKLAND

A DOLPHIN BOOK

PUBLISHED BY DOUBLEDAY

A DIVISION OF BANTAM DOUBLEDAY DELL PUBLISHING GROUP, INC.

666 FIFTH AVENUE, NEW YORK, NEW YORK 10103

DOUBLEDAY AND THE PORTRAYAL OF TWO DOLPHINS
ARE TRADEMARKS OF DOUBLEDAY, A DIVISION OF
BANTAM DOUBLEDAY DELL PUBLISHING GROUP, INC.

LIBRARY OF CONGRESS CATALOGING-IN-PUBLICATION DATA
BRODNER, STEVE
FOLD 'N' TUCK / STEVE BRODNER
P. CM.
1. CELEBRITIES — PORTRAITS — CARICATURES AND CARTOONS.
2. AMERICAN WIT AND HUMOR, PICTORIAL.   I. TITLE:
FOLD AND TUCK.
NC1429.B83A4 1990   90-3001
741.5'973 — DC20   CIP

ISBN 0-385-41164-2
PRINTED IN THE UNITED STATES OF AMERICA
SEPTEMBER 1990
FIRST EDITION

TO **ETHEL KRAMER** WHO

MADE EVERYTHING POSSIBLE

MY THANKS TO DAVID HIRSHEY, STANLEY BING, AND RIP GEORGES, WHO HELPED DEVELOP THIS CONCEPT FOR _ESQUIRE_ MAGAZINE (WHERE FOLD'N'TUCK MADE ITS DEBUT), TO _MAD_ MAGAZINE, WHICH PERMANENTLY UNHINGED MANY YOUNG MINDS, AND TO EVERY CARICATURIST WHO'S EVER TAKEN MY BREATH AWAY.

WHY FOLD 'N' TUCK?

EVER LOOK AT SOMEONE AND WONDER WHO'S REALLY LURKING UNDER THE SURFACE? IT'S BEEN MY SUSPICION THAT WE ARE ALL INHABITED BY THE SPIRITUAL RESIDUE OF MANY OTHER PEOPLE, ANIMALS, AND INANIMATE OBJECTS. THIS COULD EXPLAIN THE HUMAN CONDITION. WHAT WITH ALL THESE UNKNOWN CREATURES TEARING AROUND INSIDE US, IS IT ANY WONDER THAT PEACE AND SERENITY ARE SUCH SCARCE COMMODITIES? I HAVE, THEREFORE, TAKEN AS MY MISSION THE LIFTING OF THE VEIL ON FORTY OF THE WORLD'S MOST TORTURED SOULS. PERHAPS FOLD 'N' TUCK WILL HELP THEM FIND THE ROOTS OF THEIR PROBLEMS AND SEND THEM ON THE ROAD TO RECOVERY.

—STEVE BRODNER

HOW FOLD 'N' TUCK?

MY SUBJECTS ARE PRESENTED HERE IN DISSECTED FORM, THEIR ELEMENTS LAID VERTICALLY BEFORE YOU. TO BRING THEM TO THEIR COMBINED IDENTITY YOU NEED ONLY LIFT THE BOTTOM OF THE PAGE AND FOLD LINE B TO LINE A. THE NAME OF EACH FOLDED 'N' TUCKED FACE IS REVEALED BY LIFTING THE BOTTOM FLAP.

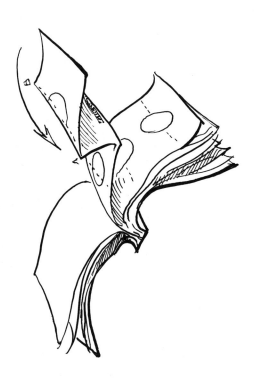

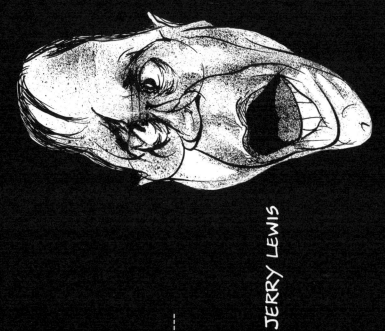

JERRY LEWIS

A

RONALD REAGAN

B

GEORGE BUSH

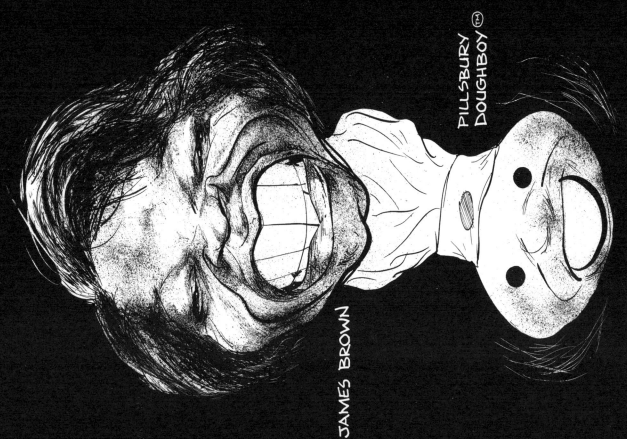

JAMES BROWN

PILLSBURY
DOUGHBOY™

OPRAH WINFREY

JOHN LENNON

A BLOWFISH

MICK JAGGER

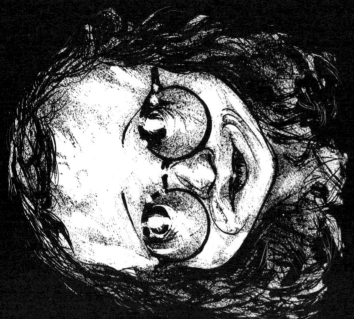

JOYCE
CAROL
OATES

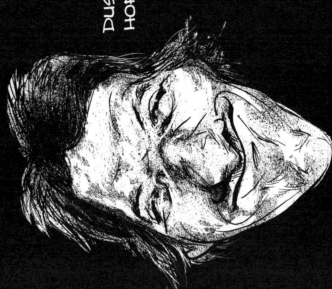

DUSTIN
HOFFMAN

WOODY ALLEN

TINA
TURNER

JACKIE GLEASON

ROSEANNE BARR

A

B

MAX
HEADROOM

HOWDY
DOODY

JOHNNY CARSON

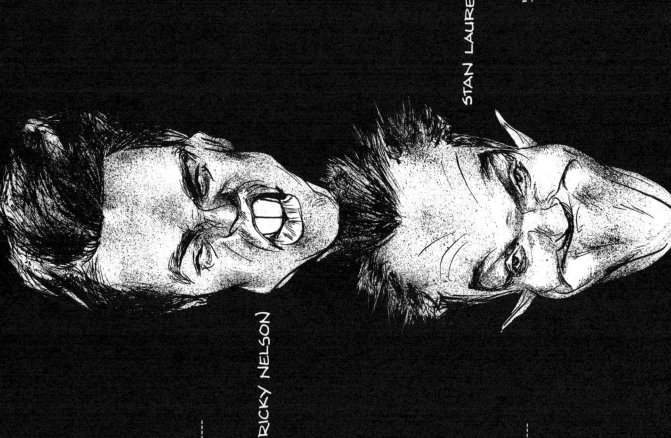

STAN LAUREL

RICKY NELSON

JAY LENO

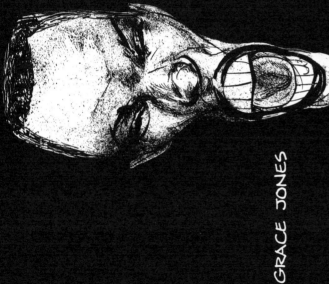

GRACE JONES

LIONEL
RICHIE

EDDIE MURPHY

IVAN BOESKY

CLARK
GABLE

TED TURNER

BESS
TRUMAN

WILLARD
SCOTT

A

B

BARBARA BUSH

DIANA ROSS

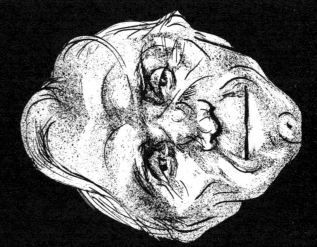

KIRK
DOUGLAS

MICHAEL JACKSON

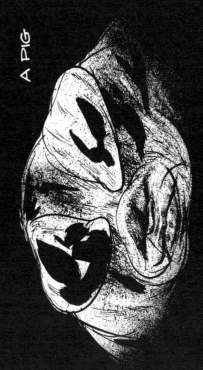

A

B

A PIG

KEVIN COSTNER

DONALD TRUMP

PEE-WEE HERMAN

KING KONG

A

B

ARNOLD SCHWARZENEGGER

A

B

PAUL
PRUDHOMME

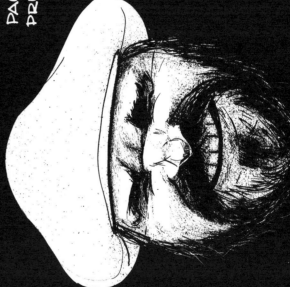

AL JOLSON

LUCIANO PAVAROTTI

A

B

ELVIS
PRESLEY

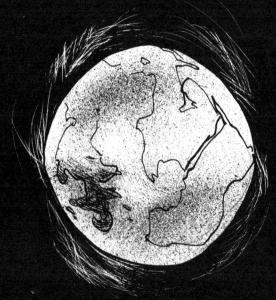

EASTERN
EUROPE

MIKHAIL GORBACHEV

BOB DYLAN

FRANK
SINATRA

A

B

BRUCE SPRINGSTEEN

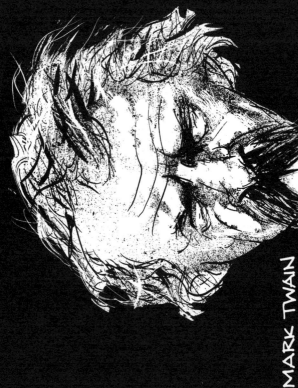

MARK TWAIN

A

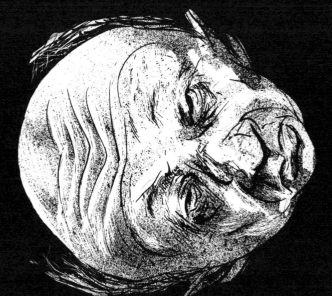

ED KOCH

B

NORMAN MAILER

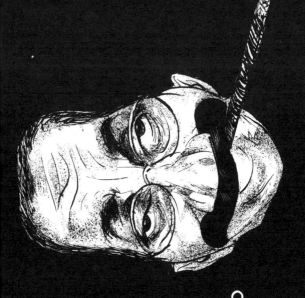

GROUCHO
MARX

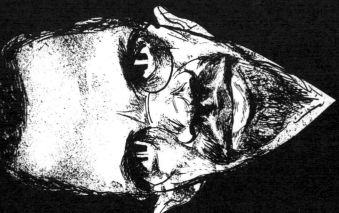

MALCOLM X

SPIKE LEE

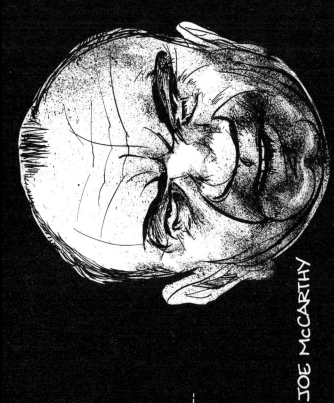

JOE McCARTHY

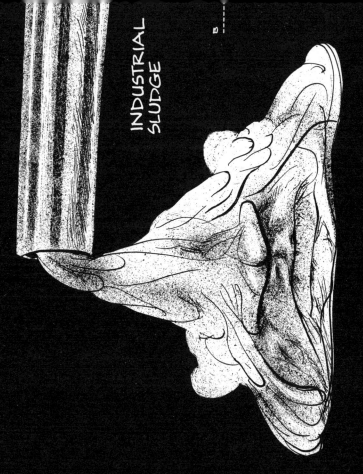

INDUSTRIAL SLUDGE

A

B

RICHARD NIXON

A

B

BARBRA
STREISAND

WILLIAM
HURT

MERYL STREEP

SHELLEY WINTERS

NANCY REAGAN

RAISA GORBACHEV

A

JIM BROWN

MARILYN
MONROE

B

JESSE JACKSON

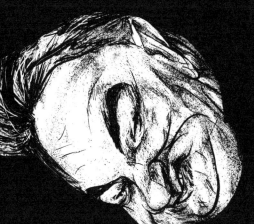

JOHN GOTTI

BERNHARD
GOETZ

HENRY KISSINGER

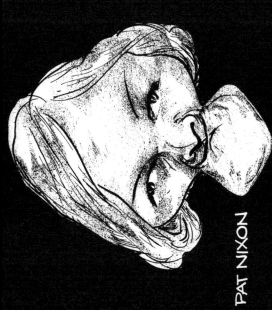

PAT NIXON

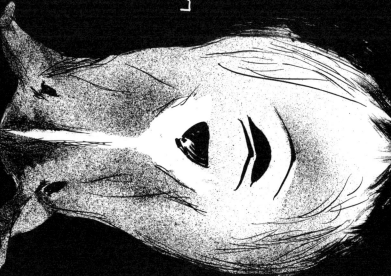

LASSIE

DIANE SAWYER

GOLDA MEIR

A

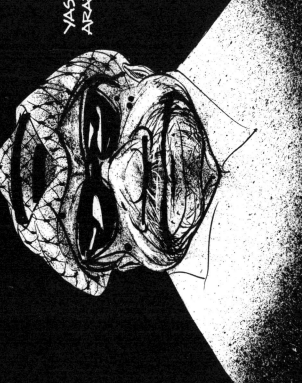

YASIR
ARAFAT

B

YITZHAK SHAMIR

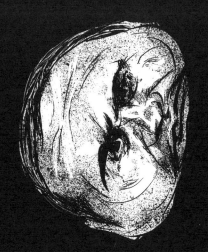

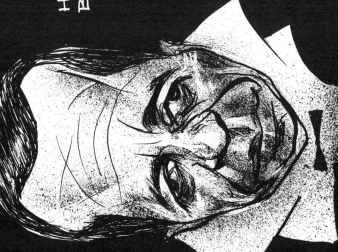

A

B

DANNY
DEVITO

HUMPHREY
BOGART

MARIO CUOMO

PRINCE

A

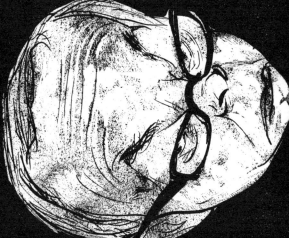

MALCOLM
FORBES

B

ELIZABETH TAYLOR

IMELDA
MARCOS

ARIEL
SHARON

PATRICK BUCHANAN

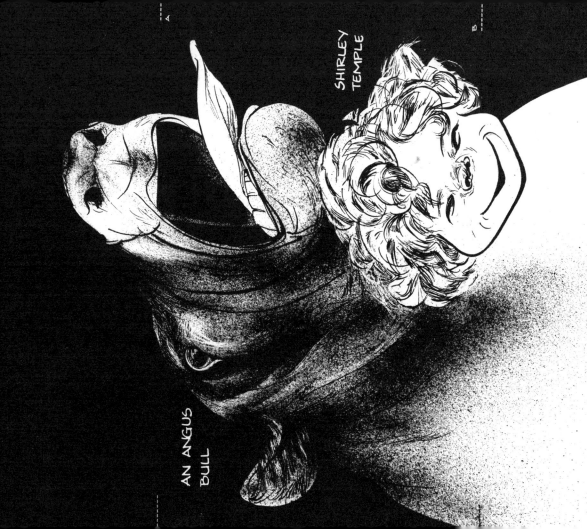

SHIRLEY TEMPLE

AN ANGUS BULL

MIKE TYSON

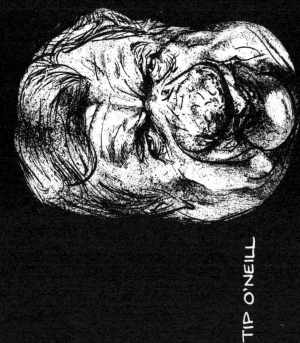

A

TIP O'NEILL

B

A STUFFED
CABBAGE

TED KENNEDY

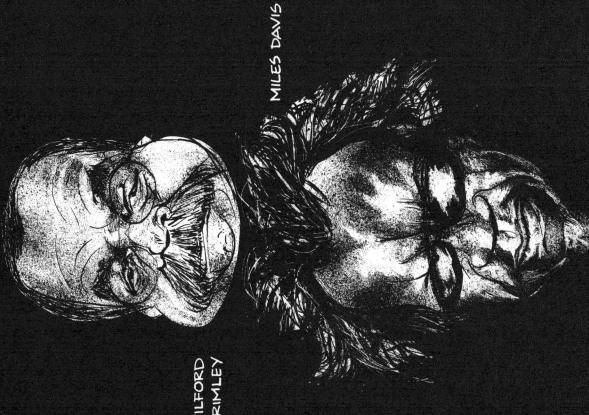

WILFORD
BRIMLEY

MILES DAVIS

A

B

BILL COSBY

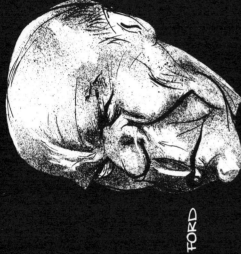

GERALD FORD

BOB HOPE

A

B

POPE JOHN PAUL II

AL PACINO

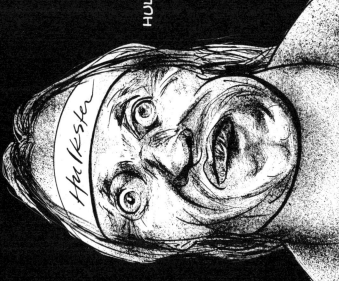

HULK HOGAN

SYLVESTER STALLONE

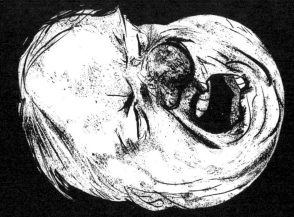

OLIVER NORTH

W.C. FIELDS

A

B

JERRY FALWELL

CLINT
EASTWOOD

ALFRED E.
NEUMAN

DAVID LETTERMAN

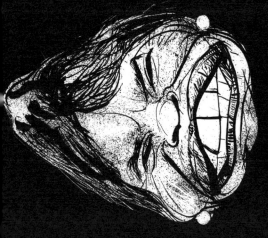

LEONA
HELMSLEY

A

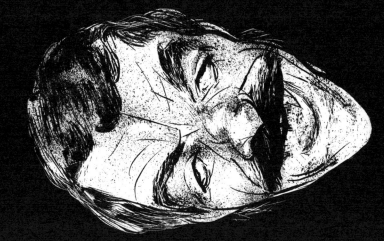

TOM
SELLECK

B

GERALDO RIVERA

GLORIA
SWANSON

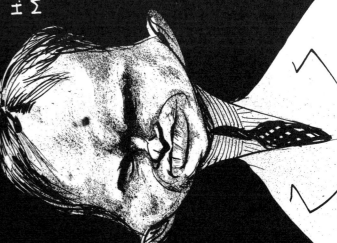

H.L.
MENCKEN

TOM WOLFE

MARGARET THATCHER

A

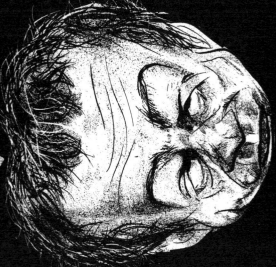

JACKIE MASON

B

TED KOPPEL

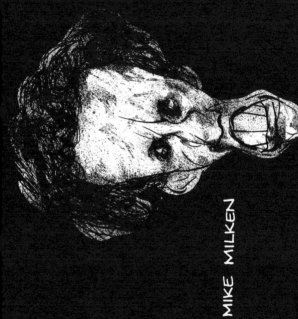

MIKE MILKEN

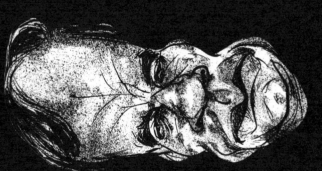

RUPERT MURDOCH

A

B

MUAMMAR QADDAFI

PRINCESS DI AND
PRINCE CHARLES

CROSS-DRESSING

DAN AND MARILYN QUAYLE